ESSENTIAL LIBRARY OF SOCIAL CHANGE

GAY RIGHTS MOVEMENT

ABDO
Publishing Company

ESSENTIAL LIBRARY OF SOCIAL CHANGE

GAY RIGHTS MOVEMENT

by Stephanie Watson

Content Consultant

Donald Haider-Markel, PhD
Department of Political Science
University of Kansas

CREDITS

Published by ABDO Publishing Company, PO Box 398166, Minneapolis, MN 55439. Copyright © 2014 by Abdo Consulting Group, Inc. International copyrights reserved in all countries. No part of this book may be reproduced in any form without written permission from the publisher. The Essential Library™ is a trademark and logo of ABDO Publishing Company.

Printed in the United States of America,
North Mankato, Minnesota
052013
092013

 THIS BOOK CONTAINS AT LEAST 10% RECYCLED MATERIALS.

Editor: Angela Wiechmann
Series Designer: Emily Love

Photo credits: Jerry Mosey/AP Images, cover, 2; Stan Honda/AFP/Getty Images, 6; NY Daily News Archive/Getty Images, 11; Fred W. McDarrah/Getty Images, 15; AFP/Getty Images, 16; Library of Congress, 21; Hulton Archive/Getty Images, 24; Stockbyte/Getty Images, 26; Photoquest/Getty Images, 28; Fred W. McDarrah/Getty Images, 31, 48; Frazer Harrison/Getty Images, 37; Grey Villet/Time Life Pictures/Getty Images, 38; Bettmann/Corbis/AP Images, 45, 68, 70; NY Daily News Archive/Getty Images, 47; Ed Kolenovsky/AP Images, 51; Peter Keegan/Authenticated News/Getty Images, 54; Jacquelyn Martin/AP Images, 57; AP Images, 58; Terry Schmitt/San Francisco Chronicle/Corbis, 64; Dave Caulkin/AP Images, 74; Scott Stewart/AP Images, 77; Shutterstock Images, 78, 93, 97; Porter Gifford/Liaison/Getty Images, 82; Thinkstock, 87; Joel Rosenbaum/The Reporter/AP Images, 88; Red Line Editorial, Inc., 100, 101

Library of Congress Control Number: 2013932971

Cataloging-in-Publication Data

Watson, Stephanie.
 Gay rights movement / Stephanie Watson.
   p. cm. -- (Essential library of social change)
Includes bibliographical references and index.
ISBN 978-1-61783-887-3
1. Gay rights--United States--Juvenile literature. 2. Gay liberation movement--United States--History--Juvenile literature. 3. Homosexuality--United states--Juvenile literature. I. Title.
305.9--dc23
                                                    2013932971

CONTENTS

CHAPTER 1

STONEWALL

T he Stonewall Inn is a nondescript two-story building sandwiched between two other nondescript buildings on Christopher Street in New York City's Greenwich Village. The bottom half of the building is brick. The top is painted white. Passersby might not give the building a second glance. But if they did happen to look up while passing this building, they would notice lines of rainbow flags waving in the breeze beneath the three second-story windows.

Rainbow flags are symbols of gay and lesbian pride. Rows of these flags hang outside the Stonewall Inn to symbolize the vital role this bar played in the gay rights movement. In fact, many people believe the events at Stonewall in the early morning hours of June 28, 1969, defined the movement.

POLICE RAID

In the 1960s, gay and lesbian people had few places where they could meet openly. New York and many other US states had laws prohibiting homosexual relations. In general, homosexuality was a social taboo. Most Americans at the time felt homosexuality was sinful and wrong. If gay people tried to congregate in public places, they faced harassment and humiliation—even physical abuse.

Gay bars were among the few places where they could meet, talk, and hang out in relative peace. Yet even gay bars were not entirely safe because they were technically against the law. To stay in business, many gay bars resorted to underhanded tactics. A Mafia man named Tony Lauria, also known as "Fat Tony," owned the Stonewall Inn. Many bars were owned by members of the Mafia, who saw the bars as a way to make a profit. It was a risky arrangement. Patrons realized the bars would likely

CHRISTOPHER STREET AND THE STONEWALL INN

Christopher Street has one of the most colorful histories of any street in New York City. It runs through the heart of eclectic Greenwich Village. It is both the oldest and longest street in that neighborhood.

Christopher Street has always been a haven for artists and creative thinkers. In the 1960s, poet Allen Ginsberg, who was gay, and folk singer Bob Dylan used to hang out at the Eighth Street Bookshop. Writers, photographers, and filmmakers gathered in Christopher Street bars. Many of the patrons were gay.

In the 1920s, all bars were illegal because the Eighteenth Amendment to the US Constitution made it illegal to sell alcohol. At that time, the first gay tearooms opened. This included Bonnie's Stone Wall, which welcomed lesbians. In the 1940s, the name changed to Bonnie's Stonewall Inn, and it became a restaurant. By the 1960s, it had transformed into Stonewall Inn, a gay club.

not exist without the Mafia's involvement. But the Mafia also blackmailed many patrons, threatening to reveal their sexuality unless they paid them large sums.

As gay bars were illegal, Mafia owners often bribed the local police to allow the bars to stay open. Despite the bribes, police sometimes conducted undercover operations to determine if a bar was frequented by gay people. Officers would come into a bar pretending to be gay. Any man who flirted back with an officer was promptly arrested. Sometimes the police would launch a raid on a bar.

In the early morning hours of Saturday, June 28, 1969, a group of plainclothes detectives and a uniformed officer entered the Stonewall Inn. The dark, two-room bar was packed with people. Many of them danced to music pouring from the jukebox. Scanning the room, the officers saw some women dressed as men in pants and button-down shirts and some men dressed as women in high heels, dresses, and makeup.

Then other officers entered the bar and announced they were closing the bar because it was selling alcohol without a license. Then they emptied the bar, leading everyone out onto Christopher Street. The officers put some of the patrons into vans to be taken to the police station.

STARTING A RIOT

What happened next is a matter of debate. "A number of incidents were happening simultaneously," said gay rights activist Craig L. Rodwell, who participated in the Stonewall riot. "There was no one thing that happened or one person, there was just . . . a flash of group, of mass anger."[1] Some accounts indicate the police were trying to arrest a woman and force her into a patrol car. When she resisted, the officers threw her into the car. This triggered the Stonewall patrons and gathering passersby to shout,

VOICES OF THE MOVEMENT

A Stonewall Inn patron, Morty Manford, describes the scene inside the club during the police raid and the growing tension outside the building that eventually exploded into a riot:

"Some men in suits and ties entered the place and walked around a little bit. Then whispers went around that the place was being raided. Suddenly, the lights were turned up and the doors were sealed, and all the patrons were held captive until the police decided what they were going to do. Everybody was anxious, not knowing whether we were going to be arrested or what was going to happen. . . . People who did not have identification or were under age and all transvestites were detained. . . . As people were released, they stayed outside. They didn't run away. They waited for their friends to come out. People who were walking up and down Christopher Street . . . also assembled. The crowd in front of the Stonewall grew and grew. And the tension started to grow." [2]

As a crowd gathered outside the Stonewall Inn, tension grew until a riot ignited.

"Police brutality!" and "Pigs!" (a slang term for police officers).[3]

Whatever the cause, suddenly people in the crowd started throwing pennies, nickels, and quarters at the officers. By throwing money, they were mocking the payoffs Mafia owners gave the police. And then bottles, cans, and rocks flew through the air at the officers and at the Stonewall Inn. Windows shattered. Someone poured lighter fluid inside the bar and set it ablaze with several officers still inside. The quiet evening had turned into a full-scale riot.

LISKER'S COVERAGE OF STONEWALL

When *New York Daily News* reporter Jerry Lisker covered the Stonewall riots for the July 6, 1969, edition, members of the gay community found his writing condescending and insulting. In his article "Homo Nest Raided, Queen Bees Are Stinging Mad," he mocked the event and its participants. *Queen Bees* was a reference to drag queens, or men (often gay men) who dress as women for theatric effect.

"The Queens pranced out to the street blowing kisses and waving to the crowd," he wrote.[7] He claimed one drag queen was less worried about the riots and more worried about the officer seeing "her" hair up in curlers. He described the moment when the riots erupted: "Queen Power exploded with all the fury of a gay atomic bomb. Queens, princesses and ladies-in-waiting began hurling anything they could get their polished, manicured fingernails on."[8] Lisker's writing minimized the importance of the Stonewall riots and belittled its participants.

As word of the riot spread through Greenwich Village, the crowd swelled to hundreds of people. They started chanting, "Gay power!"[4]

The Tactical Patrol Force, a New York Police Department riot squad, was finally called in to calm the disturbance. At 3:30 a.m., approximately two hours after the raid started, Christopher Street was quiet again. Thirteen people had been arrested.[5] A few people had been injured.[6]

But the Stonewall incident was not over yet. For the next five days, protesters kept returning to the scene of the Stonewall riot. At times, the crowd swelled to as many as 2,000 people.[9] They handed out leaflets titled "Get the Mafia and cops out of gay bars!"[10] People held hands in solidarity as police and Tactical Patrol Force officers looked on. The participants in this protest did not know it yet, but their actions during that summer week in 1969 would come to symbolize—and revolutionize—the gay rights movement.

THE BIRTH OF THE GAY RIGHTS MOVEMENT

Historian and gay rights activist Martin Duberman called Stonewall "the emblematic event in modern gay and lesbian history."[11] It was not the first time gay and lesbian people had come

HOMOSEXUAL OR GAY?

In the 1800s, German psychologist Karoly Maria Benkert coined the term *homosexual* from the Greek word *homos* ("same") and the Latin word *sexus* ("sex"). At the time, the word had a negative connotation. By the mid-1900s, people began referring to themselves as *gay*. This may have come from the French word *gaie*. It literally means "gay," or "happy," but it was also used in Europe as slang in the 1800s to describe homosexual men.

Although *gay* can refer to men or women, it most often refers to men. Homosexual women are often called *lesbians*, named for the Greek island Lesbos, home of the ancient Greek lesbian poet Sappho. *Bisexual* describes a person attracted to both sexes. And *transgender* refers to people who identify with or express a gender other than their biological sex. Today, the entire gay community is often represented by the acronym GLBT, for "gay, lesbian, bisexual, and transgender."

together to advocate for their rights. But it was the first time they had fought back so forcefully and aggressively. It was also the first time a gay protest was covered in the news media.

Although the gay rights movement did not start with Stonewall, it is considered a defining moment. Stonewall galvanized the gay and lesbian movement across the country. Within the next few years, several gay rights groups formed. Gay-focused newspapers, bookstores, and churches sprang up. The fight for gay civil rights was officially under way. ●

**In the days following the riots, people »
celebrated outside the Stonewall Inn.**

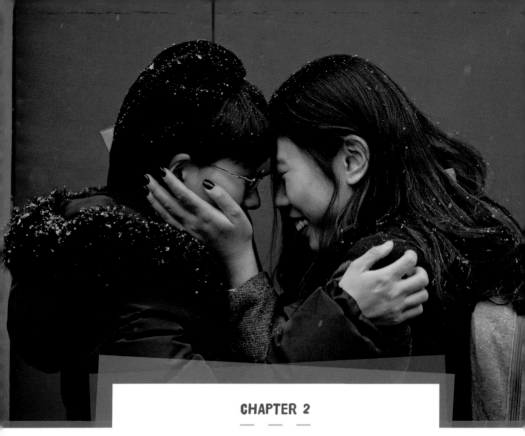

CHAPTER 2

A TIME OF DARKNESS

Same-sex attraction has been written about since the earliest civilizations. Ancient Greek and Roman literature includes many tales of love between men. In his *Symposium* text, dating to approximately 380 BCE, Greek philosopher Plato even suggests an army be made up entirely of same-sex lovers, reasoning that "a state or army which was made up only of lovers and their loves would be invincible. For love will convert the veriest coward into an inspired hero."[1]

With the end of the Roman Empire and the introduction of Christianity came a less permissive attitude about same-sex love. Any sex not solely for procreation was considered sinful—a crime against nature. Today, many Christians cite passages from the Bible as justification for labeling homosexuality as immoral and wrong. One of the most quoted passages is from the Book of Leviticus: "You shall not lie with a man as with a woman: that is an abomination."[2]

CENTURIES OF PREJUDICE AND PERSECUTION

Despite religious objections, gay people were allowed to live in relative peace until approximately the 1300s. Then the Catholic Church began to forbid homosexual sex and treat it as a crime. In parts of Europe, men could be executed for having sex with other men. Under the leadership of King Henry VIII in the 1530s, British lawmakers approved the Buggery Act. According to the new law, men engaging in homosexual relations could be put to death. The United States also did not offer equality for its gay citizens. At the time the Declaration of Independence was signed in 1776, all 13 of the original colonies made homosexuality a crime with the penalty of death.[3] The Puritans in New Haven, Connecticut, had a statute in their legal code that read, "If any man lyeth with mankinde, as a man lyeth with a woman, both of them have committed abomination, they both shall surely be put to death."[4]

Change was slow. It was only after the American Revolution (1775–1783) that states began repealing the death penalty. However, they still imposed prison sentences for people convicted of being gay. It was not until the mid-1800s that all the states had removed the death penalty as a punishment for being gay. Other countries also began changing their laws around the same time.

Even as laws became slightly more permissive, it was still dangerous to be openly gay. That was why most gay people chose to stay silent about their sexual orientation. English writer Oscar Wilde, who was persecuted for being gay in the 1800s, called it "the Love that dare not speak its name."[5] Part of the reason for the hatred and persecution was a lack of understanding about what caused homosexuality or what it meant to be gay. That attitude would begin to change in the early 1900s.

EARLY STUDIES ON HOMOSEXUALITY

Scientists and doctors did not study homosexuality until the late 1800s. But once researchers delved into the topic of same-sex attraction, some of them formed new theories about it. According to the new way of thinking, gay people were not criminals or immoral. Instead, they were considered mentally ill. In his 1894 book *Psychopathia Sexualis* German psychiatrist Richard Krafft-Ebing described homosexuality as a disease. Because they were considered "sick," many gay people were committed to mental institutions in the late 1800s and early 1900s.

British doctor Henry Havelock Ellis,

GAY "TREATMENTS"

In the late 1800s, the idea that homosexuality was a mental illness began to circulate in the medical community. This led to treatments, called conversion therapy, which attempted to "cure" gay people.

Some of the earliest attempts involved vigorous exercise. Other methods were much harsher. In one treatment, gay people were forced to watch sexual images featuring people of the same sex. Then they were given shocks, forced to throw up, or beaten. The idea was these methods would force gay people to feel disgust for same-sex acts.

Conversion therapy is still tried today, although it is used more by religious groups than by doctors. The American Psychological Association has taken the position that "homosexuality is not a mental disorder and thus is not something that needs to or can be 'cured.'"[6] The American Psychiatric Association and many other medical organizations have also spoken out against the practice.

Austrian psychoanalyst Sigmund Freud, and German physician Magnus Hirschfeld had a more accepting view of homosexuality. In his 1896 book, *Sexual Inversion*, Ellis argues that people are born gay. In other words, they cannot control their attraction to people of the same sex. Freud believed everyone is born bisexual, or attracted to members of both sexes. He said people only become gay or straight, also known as heterosexual, later in life because of their family environment. Freud's attitude is evident in this letter he wrote to the mother of a gay son: "Homosexuality is assuredly no advantage, but it is nothing to be ashamed of, no vice, no degradation, it cannot be classified as an illness."[7]

In 1919, Hirschfeld opened the Institute for Sexual Science in Berlin, Germany. It was the first research facility devoted to the study of sexuality. The institute housed thousands of documents and photos related to sexual issues, including homosexuality. In 1933, after the Nazis took over power in Germany, they destroyed the institute and burned all its documents.

Despite Ellis's, Hirschfeld's, and Freud's sympathetic take on homosexuality, many people still held to the idea it was a disease. This led to attempts to "treat" people who were gay. Those treatments ranged from simple methods such as talk therapy to extreme methods such as electroshock therapy or even brain surgery.

Sigmund Freud was one of several physicians
and psychologists who disagreed with the
notion that homosexuality was an illness.

SOCIETY FOR HUMAN RIGHTS

Before World War II (1939–1945), gay people in Europe
and the United States experienced gains as well as
setbacks. Places such as Berlin and Greenwich Village

became centers of gay society in the 1920s. Even though gay people could still be persecuted, they were able to enjoy some freedom. They often gathered at the gay nightclubs that were popping up in these and other cities.

On December 10, 1924, Bavarian-born Henry Gerber founded the first gay rights organization in the United States. Called the Society for Human Rights, the group was based in Chicago, Illinois. It published the *Friendship and Freedom* newsletter, which reported on the society's efforts to change antigay laws. Just a year later, police raided Gerber's home and seized the society's materials. He was arrested. Although he was eventually released from jail, Gerber lost his job at the post office and was forced to shut down the society.

MORE RESEARCH

The decades that followed were not much easier for gay people. In 1948, biologist Alfred Kinsey published a landmark book called *Sexual Behavior in the Human Male*. He reported that 37 percent of white male adults had had at least one sexual experience with another male.[9] The finding suggested more men were gay or engaging in homosexual relations than anyone had thought. In the early 1950s, psychologist Evelyn Hooker conducted a study

GRANDFATHER OF THE GAY RIGHTS MOVEMENT

Henry Gerber was born in Bavaria in 1895. In 1913, he moved to the United States. Just a few years after arriving, he was briefly committed to a mental institution for being gay. When the United States entered World War I (1914–1918) in 1917, he served as a member of the US military in Germany. While there, he read a gay publication and was inspired by the relative freedom gay men had at the time in Germany.

When he returned to the United States after the war, Gerber started his own organization, the Society for Human Rights. He used his own money to run the society. He said he was "willing to slave and suffer and risk losing my job and savings and even my liberty for the ideal."[10]

Although the group he founded did not last very long, Gerber is considered by many people to be the grandfather of the gay rights movement.

of gay men. She found that not only were gay men as mentally fit as straight men, but that it was impossible for medical doctors or psychologists to tell the difference between men who were gay and those who were straight.

Instead of improving conditions, these findings came at a very difficult time for gay people in US history. In the 1950s, the US government was suspicious of Communists and anyone with secrets to hide. The witch hunt against gays was beginning. ●

« **Alfred Kinsey's research findings suggested a higher amount of same-sex activity than most people suspected.**

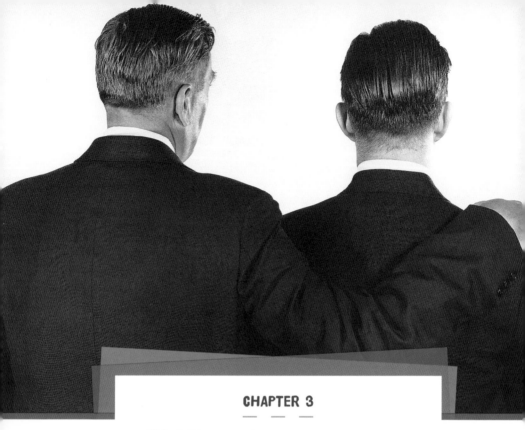

CHAPTER 3

THE HOMOPHILE
MOVEMENT

During the first half of the 1900s, gay people could fly under the radar in the United States. They could work and go about their lives, as long as they stayed in the "closet," a term used to describe gay, lesbian, bisexual, or transgender people who do not disclose their sexual orientation.

But times changed. In the 1950s, citizens and government officials clung tightly to what they felt were

« **During the 1950s, gay people working for the government were the targets of persecution.**

traditional values about family, religion, patriotism, and morality. They were fearful and mistrustful of anyone who did not conform to those values.

Two things happened in the 1950s that made life very difficult for gay people in the United States. First, Kinsey released his report showing more people engaged in homosexual behavior than had been thought previously. And second, the spread of communism in Eastern Europe after World War II made many US lawmakers paranoid and suspicious about who might be hiding in their midst.

ANTISODOMY LAWS

Living as a gay person in the United States in the 1950s was more than frowned upon. In most states, it was illegal. Every state in the country had a law against sodomy. These laws made it illegal to have the kind of sexual relations same-sex partners could have with one another—the kind of sex that could not produce a baby. Although some antisodomy laws did apply to opposite-sex couples, they were usually targeted specifically at gays. If two consenting adults of the same sex were found together in their own bed in their own home, they could be arrested. Some states began doing away with antisodomy laws in the 1960s and 1970s. But 14 other states upheld these laws until a 2003 Supreme Court ruling overturned them.[1]

Officials such as Senator Joseph McCarthy targeted gay government employees in the 1950s.

THE WITCH HUNT

The US government reacted forcefully. Senator Joseph McCarthy—who was already hunting for Communists in the US government and society—led the charge against gay people working in the government.

Two committees formed to address the employment of gays in government jobs. Senators Clyde Hoey and Kenneth S. Wherry chaired the committees. The Hoey Committee released a report in December 1950 entitled "Employment of Homosexuals and Other Sex Perverts in Government." The committees concluded gay people were not good candidates for government jobs because of their "lack of emotional stability" and "the weakness of their moral fiber."[2] Lawmakers believed gay employees might be easy to blackmail, especially by Communists, because they were nervous about their sexual orientation being revealed.

J. EDGAR HOOVER

Federal Bureau of Investigation (FBI) director J. Edgar Hoover was one of the most outspoken members of the government's assault on gay people in the federal workforce. In 1937, Hoover declared a "War on the Sex Criminal," which he considered to be "the most loathsome of all the vast army of crime."[3]

Although he led this crackdown, Hoover may have been keeping his own secret. Throughout his career, he had a very close relationship with his assistant, Clyde Tolson. The two men spent extensive time together. They were rumored to be in love. There were also unproven rumors that Hoover sometimes dressed in women's clothing.

Could the FBI director have been gay? If he had been, it would have certainly ruined his career. Some people think his aggressive attack against gay people was an attempt to hide his own secret.

In 1953, President Dwight D. Eisenhower issued an executive order listing "sexual perversion" as a basis to be barred from a job.[4] The Morals Division of the Metropolitan Police in Washington, DC, set up a so-called Perversion Squad to root out gay employees. Members of the squad spied upon suspected gay people and opened their mail. As the government fired gay employees, private companies began doing the same.

HARRY HAY AND THE MATTACHINE SOCIETY

In the 1950s, there was little to no support for gay people in the United States. There were no societies they could turn to. They had no celebrities with whom they could identify. And there were no marches where they could proclaim their pride and solidarity. Gay people faced loneliness, isolation, and prejudice. They could be sent to mental hospitals or fired from their jobs because of their sexual orientation.

Some gay Americans became fed up with this treatment and decided they wanted to change things. One of those people was Harry Hay. Hay was a Communist and a gay rights pioneer concerned about the way the government was purging gay people from their jobs. In 1951, he founded the Mattachine Society. The name had symbolic meaning. Mattachines were unmarried

As the first gay rights group, the Mattachine Society challenged discrimination in places such as bars.

French men who danced in masks at festivals during the Middle Ages.

Mattachine was a homophile organization, meaning it supported the rights and social acceptance of gays and lesbians. By 1952, the Mattachine Society had approximately 5,000 members.[5] The group worked to help gay people assimilate into society through education and connections with sympathetic allies in the straight community.

In 1953, members of the society ousted Hay because they worried about his Communist background at a time when the country was decidedly anticommunist. They reorganized under the leadership of journalist Hal Call and accountant Donald Lucas.

The Mattachine Society moved its headquarters to San Francisco, California. It began publishing the *Mattachine Review*

HARRY HAY

Harry Hay, who would become one of the earliest leaders in the gay rights movement, was born on April 7, 1912, in Sussex, England. His parents were American, and the family returned to the United States five years after his birth.

In the late 1930s and 1940s, Hay worked as an actor in the film and theater industry. He was also an active member of the Communist Party. Being gay as well as Communist put him in double danger when the government began its purge of both groups in the early 1950s.

Hay founded the Mattachine Society in 1951. Within two years, the group had grown and changed. Even after being ousted from Mattachine, Hay stayed active in the gay community. In the 1970s, he and his partner, John Burnside, moved to New Mexico and brought the gay liberation movement with them. Hay died on October 24, 2002, at age 90, a legend in the gay rights movement.

journal. Society chapters sprang up around the country, including in New York and Philadelphia, Pennsylvania.

Despite its quick expansion, the Mattachine Society did not last long. By 1961, the national organization dissolved, although some city chapters continued. However, its contributions lived on. The group is credited with officially launching the gay rights movement.

ONE

While the Mattachine Society was still in existence, its Los Angeles, California, chapter made another big contribution to the gay rights movement. In 1953, the chapter published the magazine *One*. The name came from a quote by British writer Thomas Carlyle: "A mystic bond of brotherhood makes all men one."[6] It was also a reference to the way gay people sometimes referred to each other: "He's one."[7]

The magazine operated out of a tiny two-room office. Because magazine distributors refused to carry *One*, staff members themselves had to distribute the publication to subscribers. Yet even under these difficult circumstances, there was a real sense of pride. "You could be proud of being yourself. That in itself was radical. Nobody put it in words, but that was the underlying thought and underlying feeling behind the magazine," said Martin Block, one of its founders.[8]

CHALLENGES OF THE GAY RIGHTS MOVEMENT

The mid-1900s were a time of major social upheaval in the United States. African Americans were fighting for their civil rights. Women were championing equality issues. And gay people were trying to end the prejudice and discrimination they had faced for centuries.

But gay rights have been in many ways more difficult to achieve than other groups' rights. First, people against gay rights have often argued that being gay is a choice, unlike one's sex or race. At a 1980 hearing, Reverend Charles A. McIlhenny of the First Orthodox Presbyterian Church in San Francisco testified that gay people are not a "bona fide minority" because "homosexual behavior can be changed if the individual really desires a change."[11] Also, the gay rights movement has not had one leader who inspired the masses, such as Martin Luther King Jr. did for civil rights.

Despite these challenges, the gay rights movement has slowly and steadily moved closer to its goal of achieving full civil rights for all gay people.

Because it contained information and news about gay people, *One* had to be mailed in secret. The staff assumed the government would consider it obscene and not allow it to be mailed. The 1,650 subscribers received their monthly copies in plain envelopes.[9] They were marked only by a return address: 232 South Hill Street, Los Angeles.

Despite the secrecy, it was not long before the US post office caught on to what was in the plain envelopes. In October 1954, a Los Angeles post office branch seized 600 copies of the magazine.[10] After reviewing the content, government censors banned *One*, deeming it too "obscene, lewd, lascivious, or filthy" to be carried through the mail system.[12]

The magazine fought back, filing a lawsuit in federal court against the Los Angeles postmaster. On January 13, 1958, the US Supreme Court ruled *One* was not obscene just because it dealt with gay material. It was a landmark victory, paving the way for other gay publications to be sent through the mail.

DAUGHTERS OF BILITIS

By the mid-1950s, the country's first lesbian rights organization also launched. It was called the Daughters of Bilitis, after Pierre Louÿs's lesbian-themed love poems, "Songs of Bilitis," from the 1800s. Phyllis Lyon and Del Martin started the group as a small community of lesbians who gathered secretly for companionship and conversation.

In 1956, the Daughters of Bilitis started its own magazine, the *Ladder*. By 1960, the group had expanded, forming chapters in Chicago, Los Angeles, and New York. The Daughters of Bilitis hosted dances, suppers, and meetings. They had speakers covering topics such as how to come out to friends and family members.

The Daughters of Bilitis organization was another small victory for the gay rights movement, but more challenges would lie ahead. The witch hunt for gays working in the government would continue for several years, especially in Washington, DC. Thousands would lose their jobs. Then in the late 1950s, the first individual would stand up against the discrimination and lead others in the fight. ●

In 2004, Phyllis Lyon, *left*, and Del Martin, *right*, » cofounders of the Daughters of Bilitis, were recognized for their work as gay rights pioneers.

CHAPTER 4

THE FIRST FIGHT BACK

T he 1960s were a time of great social and political upheaval in the United States. It was the decade of the civil rights movement and Vietnam War protests. Yet even before these mass demonstrations were in full swing, a few brave gay people began standing up to assert their rights and protest their treatment in government and society.

At the head of this charge was Harvard-educated astronomer Franklin Kameny. On December 20, 1957, Kameny was fired from his position with the Army Map Service because he was gay. A year later, the Civil Service Commission— the agency that oversees government jobs— barred him from holding or seeking any federal job for a period of three years.

Kameny was one of an estimated 5,000 gay people who were fired from their government jobs in the early 1950s.[1] What set him apart was that he decided to take a stand against the

LAVENDER SCARE

Lavender Scare is a term used to describe the persecution and firing of gays and lesbians from government jobs from the late 1940s to the late 1960s. To justify these firings, the government described gays and lesbians as "perverts" who were a threat to traditional values.

When suspected gay people were pinpointed, the FBI brought them in for questioning—usually without lawyers present. FBI agents would threaten to expose anyone who refused to cooperate. Officers would say things such as, "We have your friend in the next room. She's already told us you're gay. You give us the names of others and we'll go easier on you."[2]

Although the witch hunt against gays and lesbians ended in the late 1960s, gay people could still be fired from government jobs. That finally changed in 1998, when President Bill Clinton signed an executive order banning discrimination based on sexual orientation in the federal civilian workforce.

Civil Service Commission. "I took that as a declaration of war against me and my fellow gays and became the first person, to my knowledge, to fight back on this issue," he said.[3]

KAMENY FIGHTS BACK

Kameny began by appealing his case to the chairman of the Civil Service Commission. That got him nowhere. In June 1959, he took his case to federal court. It was dismissed. When he appealed to the US Court of Appeals for the District of Columbia, the judges upheld the previous court's decision. Through this time, he was still unemployed. To make matters worse, his attorney, Byron Scott, dropped the case because he considered it a lost cause.

Still, Kameny refused to give up. On January 21, 1961, he took his case all the way to the US Supreme Court. It was the first time a gay rights case had been argued there. Kameny wrote his own petition, in which he argued, "Our government exists to protect and assist *all* of its citizens, not, as in the case of homosexuals, to harm, to victimize, and to destroy them."[4] He called the government's actions in firing him an "affront to human dignity."[5] Despite Kameny's efforts, the Supreme Court also denied his case.

Next, Kameny founded the Washington, DC, chapter of the Mattachine Society in 1961. From

VOICES OF THE MOVEMENT

In a book published in 2006, gay rights pioneer Franklin Kameny reflects on his role in the movement and on its evolution:

❝These days, some people call me a father or grandfather of the gay movement. I have my ego, and I'm very glad to be called that, but I wasn't alone. There were people who preceded me. I guess we saw the trails and blazed them. We pushed against a sometimes willing, and sometimes a very unwilling, larger mass, but I never thought that it was possible that the movement would become as large as it is today. Things have moved so quickly. Even as late as ten years ago, there were few of us who would have expected that we would be where we are now.❞ 6

there, he launched efforts to overturn the government's antigay policies. In the summer of 1962, the society began a letter-writing campaign. The Mattachine Society of Washington then reached out for help from the local chapter of the American Civil Liberties Union (ACLU), an organization that advocates for civil rights. The ACLU eventually agreed to take on their case. After a long effort, the Mattachine Society, with the ACLU's help, finally won *Scott v. Macy* (1965) and *Norton v. Macy* (1969), two court battles for employees who had been fired for their sexual orientation.

LETTER-WRITING CAMPAIGN

In 1962, Kameny and the Mattachine Society of Washington began a letter-writing campaign. Society members wrote to every senator, representative, and Supreme Court justice, as well as to President John F. Kennedy and his cabinet. They asked each government official for a face-to-face meeting in which they could discuss their objections to government job discrimination. The only two representatives who agreed were William Fitts Ryan of New York and Robert Nix of Pennsylvania. To many of their letters, the Mattachine members received nasty responses, such as "all homosexuals are unstable," and "homosexuals are not suitable for appointment."[7]

FIRST GAY RIGHTS PROTESTS

While he was fighting for gay employment rights in the US court system, Kameny was also leading the first gay rights protests with fellow activists such as Barbara Gittings, who had founded the New York chapter of the Daughters of Bilitis.

On April 17, 1965, Kameny led a group of approximately ten protesters in front of the White House.[8] They carried signs that read, "Homosexuals Ask for the Right to the Pursuit of Happiness."[9] The protesters called on the White House to stop discriminating against gays in the federal workforce. Protesters dressed conservatively— suits and ties for men

TWO LANDMARK COURT CASES

Kameny and the Mattachine Society of Washington helped win two important court cases in the late 1960s. In the first case, *Scott v. Macy*, Bruce Scott had been denied a job with the Defense Department because of what the department called "immoral conduct."[10] In 1965, the US court of appeals ruled the charge was too vague. It said the Civil Service Commission, under chairman John Macy, had never explained exactly what conduct it found to be immoral.

The second case, *Norton v. Macy*, involved Clifford Norton. He had been fired from his job at NASA when he was caught driving around a park with another man. The Washington, DC, circuit court ruled that being a homosexual did not affect Norton's ability to do his job, and therefore he could not be fired for it. Although these cases were not fought in the Supreme Court, they were major victories for gay people in the workforce.

and dresses for women. They wanted to be seen by the straight community as normal and respectable. The rules for picketing stated, "to gain acceptance, new ideas must be clothed in familiar garb."[11]

Between 1965 and 1969, the protests expanded to the Pentagon and the State Department in Washington, DC, as well as to locations in New York City and Philadelphia. Openly demonstrating in public was considered a brave act in the 1960s, a time when few gay people were "out." "Those early pickets were scary. It was scary because there were so few of us who could take the risk of being so public," said Gittings.[12] Marchers feared their employers would happen to turn on the evening news, see them at the protest, and then fire them. They also feared they would be harassed by onlookers.

In 1965, activist Craig Rodwell of New York's Mattachine Society helped launch a yearly event that became known as the Annual Reminder. Each July 4, a group of gay activists silently marched outside Philadelphia's Independence Hall. According to Rodwell, the protest was a "reminder that a group of Americans still don't have their basic rights to life, liberty, and the pursuit of happiness."[13] It was a patriotic attempt to earn the same rights for gay US citizens that straight citizens already enjoyed.

Wearing formal suits and dresses, gay rights activists stage a 1965 protest in front of the White House.

As the protests continued across the country, the gay rights movement became better organized and gained momentum. In 1966, 15 different gay organizations joined forces to form the North American Conference of Homophile Organizations (NACHO).[14] The group challenged antigay policies in the workforce and the military. At a 1968 conference in Chicago, NACHO adopted the official slogan, "Gay is Good."[15]

The riot that erupted at Greenwich Village's Stonewall Inn on June 28, 1969, turned the entire nation's attention to the struggle and reinvigorated the fight for gay rights. As a result of Stonewall, gay activists created several new and more outspoken organizations. After that landmark 1969 event, "we could say who we are and in the unifying power of our speech, fight back," said gay rights activist Cindy Patton.[16]

On the twentieth anniversary of the Stonewall » riots, members of the gay community reflect upon the event's impact decades later.

CHAPTER 5

LAUNCH OF THE GAY RIGHTS MOVEMENT

A fter the Stonewall riots in June 1969, the gay rights movement experienced a radical shift. Gone were the conformist suits and ties they had worn to protest marches. Gone were the calm pleas to integrate into society.

In July 1969, a month after the riots, the Annual Reminder protest moved from Philadelphia to New York. It was renamed Christopher Street Liberation Day. In 1970, it turned into a gay pride parade. At first, a few hundred people would gather on Christopher Street to commemorate the Stonewall riots. But within a few years, the parade had spread to other cities and attracted thousands of marchers.[1] Today, gay pride parades are held all over the world each summer.

NEW ACTIVIST GROUPS FORM

Stonewall inspired many people to band together and take up the cause of gay rights. Many of the new gay rights organizations were openly radical. They wanted to wipe away the old societal norms. They proudly stepped out of the closet and demanded a country in which gay people had complete freedom and equality.

First among these organizations was the Gay Liberation Front (GLF), started in July 1969 by activists John O'Brien, Jim Fouratt, Martha Shelley, and others. Some of the GLF's founders also had protested against the Vietnam War. The GLF's statement of purpose read, "We are a revolutionary group of men and women, formed with the realization that complete sexual liberation for

ZAPS

Gay groups such as the GLF found a new way to get attention—through a practice they called "zaps." They would show up at political meetings or other events and do something outrageous to get the media's and officials' attentions.

Just before the November 1969 mayoral election in New York City, 13 members of the Gay Commandoes, which were part of the GLF, sneaked into a debate between the candidates. Commando Marty Robinson challenged the conservative candidate, Mario Procaccino. He said, "It's 1776, Mr. Procaccino. The homosexual revolution has begun."[4]

In 1970, the Gay Activists Alliance (GAA) launched another zap, this one against *Harper's* magazine. It was in response to an article by Joseph Epstein. GAA members showed up at *Harper's* New York office on October 27. They set up a table in the reception area, served coffee and donuts, and greeted every employee by saying, "Good morning, I'm a homosexual. We're here to protest the Epstein article. Would you like some coffee?"[5]

all people cannot come about unless existing social institutions are abolished."[2]

The GLF's name was modeled after the National Liberation Front, a South Vietnamese political organization that fought against the United States and the South Vietnamese government during the Vietnam War. They were heroes to US liberals, who opposed the Vietnam War. "It was David against Goliath, fighting for their nation and for the liberation of their people, daring to stand up to the most powerful army in the world," said GLF founder Shelley.[3] The GLF stood up

Inspired by Stonewall, radical activist groups such as the Gay Liberation Front fought for change.

for more than just gay rights. It also supported several other leftist movements, including the Black Panthers (a militant African-American group) and the anti–Vietnam War movement.

The GLF did not appeal to every gay activist. Some found it too radical. Others felt the group diluted its message by supporting other causes. Alienated members of the GLF formed their own organizations. One of these was the Gay Activists Alliance (GAA), founded in 1969. Instead of fighting back against established society, the GAA's goal was to reform the law by working within the political system. The group lobbied to repeal antisodomy laws, end police harassment, and stop employment and housing discrimination.

THE FIREHOUSE

In May 1971, the GAA opened the Firehouse, a converted Victorian firehouse on Wooster Street in New York City's SoHo neighborhood. It was not only the group's headquarters but also the first gay community center in the country. It was a gathering place for members of the local gay community.

The bright-red building hosted everything from political meetings to dances. Between 9:00 p.m. and 3:00 a.m. on Saturday nights, the four floors of the building were packed with partiers dancing to music from legendary DJ Barry Lederer.

On October 8, 1974, the Firehouse was destroyed in an arson attack. Police never found out who set the fire. The mystery remains today.

NATIONAL GAY TASK FORCE

In 1973, biologist Bruce Voeller and a group of other activists founded the National Gay Task Force (NGTF)—now called the National Gay and Lesbian Task Force. This group was more like the Mattachine Society than the radical gay rights organizations.

The NGTF wanted equal rights, but it wanted to achieve them through the mainstream political process. The NGTF was also much more structured than any organization before it. It had a board of directors and paid staff members. Among its goals were to pass antidiscrimination laws

FAMILIES SHOW THEIR SUPPORT

In the 1970s, some new groups formed to show support for their gay loved ones. Many parents had a difficult time learning their children are gay. But when Jeanne Manford's son, Morty, came out to her, she was more than accepting. "I told him that I loved him, and nothing else mattered," she said.[6] After Morty was beaten up during a gay rights rally, Manford wrote to the *New York Post*: "My son is a homosexual, and I love him."[7] She marched with her son in the 1972 gay pride parade in New York, carrying a sign that read, "Parents of Gays: Unite in Support for Our Children."[8]

Manford started a support group in 1973 for family members of gay people. Eventually, it evolved into Parents, Family, and Friends of Lesbians and Gays (PFLAG). Today, PFLAG has approximately 200,000 members and supporters around the world.[9]

and stop psychiatrists from defining homosexuality as a mental illness.

COLLEGE GAY RIGHTS GROUPS

The liberal social movement was very active on college campuses, where many students tried to start their own gay rights organizations. However, college administrations were not always as liberal as their students. In June 1970, students at the University of Kansas tried to start a branch of the GLF. University chancellor Laurence Chalmers rejected the group. His reason was that he did not believe "student activity funds should be allocated either to support or oppose the sexual proclivities of students, particularly when they might lead to violation of state law."[10] With the help of the ACLU, the student group sued the university. The Supreme Court refused to hear the case. Although it did not become an official college organization, the GLF remained active on the University of Kansas campus.

Students at other universities had greater success with their gay rights groups. In 1967, Columbia University freshman Robert Martin, who later changed his name to Stephen Donaldson, founded the nation's first Student Homophile League. A year later, students

« **The National Gay Task Force was one of the most structured activist groups of its time.**

at Stanford University started their own Homophile League chapter. Students at Stanford also founded a Gay Students' Union in 1970, which two years later won the university's support.

On campuses and in cities across the country, new activist groups formed, taking inspiration from the Stonewall riots. These new groups would lead the gay rights movement into a new era. ●

Buttons from a collection of gay rights »
memorabilia declare protest slogans.

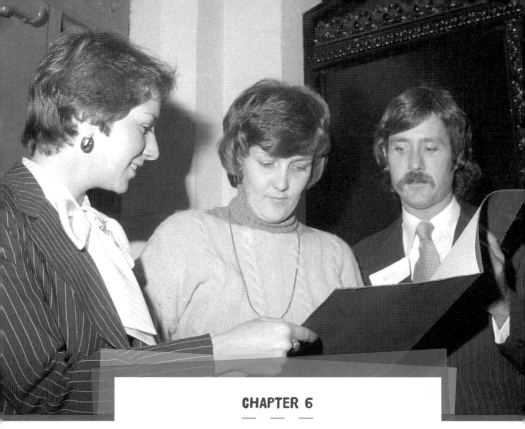

CHAPTER 6

GOING MAINSTREAM

In the early and mid-1900s, the goal of most gay people was to slip under the radar and not get noticed. Then in the 1970s, many started to come out of the closet. Not only did they live more openly, but they also played an active part in politics and society. Gay activists realized one of the best ways to change the laws restricting gay rights was to become lawmakers themselves.

The first openly gay candidate for Congress was also one of the leading voices in the early gay rights movement—Franklin Kameny. He ran for a congressional seat in Washington, DC, in 1971, but lost the election. In 1974, Kathy Kozachenko became the first openly gay person to gain political office when she won a seat on the Ann Arbor, Michigan, city council. An even greater victory came the same year when Elaine Noble won a seat in the Massachusetts House of Representatives. "People think I'm nuts," she said at the time. "But I think it can be done."[1]

Inspired by Noble's victory, sitting Minnesota state senator Allan Spear came out that December, making him the country's first openly gay male state legislator. Later, other politicians also came out, including Gerry Studds and Barney Frank, both Democratic congressmen from Massachusetts.

Of the two major political parties in the United States, the Democratic Party has historically been more sympathetic than the Republicans to the gay cause. In 1980, the Democrats became the first party to add gay civil rights to their platform. The new platform opposed discrimination based on sexual orientation. That year, the Human Rights Campaign Fund (now the Human Rights Campaign) was founded to support candidates running for political office who supported gay rights.

NO LONGER A MENTAL ILLNESS

One of the biggest hurdles the gay rights movement faced was the stigma that surrounded being gay. Beginning in the late 1800s, when scientists began studying homosexuality, it had been viewed as a mental illness. Gay rights groups spent years fighting against this misconception. At a 1971 meeting of the American Psychiatric Association (APA), Kameny grabbed the microphone and yelled, "Psychiatry has waged a relentless war of extermination against us. You may take this as a declaration of war against you."[3] Kameny was determined to make the APA

BELLA ABZUG AND THE GAY RIGHTS BILL

One of the greatest political advocates for gay rights in the 1970s was New York congresswoman Bella Abzug. Abzug was straight, but she was known for championing liberal issues and for her flamboyant style. She wore enormous floppy hats and had the kind of loud, insistent voice that "could boil the fat off a taxicab driver's neck," according to writer Norman Mailer.[2]

Abzug introduced the Equality Act of 1974, the first national gay civil rights bill. It prevented discrimination by employers, state governments, and schools on the basis of sexual orientation. Although the bill never did pass, it resurfaced two decades later in 1994 as the Employment Non-Discrimination Act. It failed to pass by two votes in 1996. It was introduced to Congress every year afterward, and it continued to gain support. In 2012, President Barack Obama said he supported passage of the bill.

change its position
on homosexuality.

In 1973, the APA
did just that. It finally
removed homosexuality
from its list of mental
disorders. Kameny
responded by joking,
"In one fell swoop, 15
million gay people were
cured!"[4]

HARVEY MILK AND THE WEST COAST MOVEMENT

Before gay candidates
gained national support,
Harvey Milk was one
of the most prominent
political figures in the
gay rights movement.
Milk began his career in
New York, supporting
the campaign
of conservative

THE MASKED GAY PSYCHIATRIST

One of the biggest efforts gay activists undertook in the early 1970s was to change the diagnosis of homosexuality as a mental illness. To do this, they relentlessly pursued the American Psychiatric Association (APA).

In 1972, Kameny and Gittings were asked to speak to an APA panel on homosexuality called "Psychiatry: Friend or Foe to Homosexuals?" Gittings felt it was important to have a gay psychiatrist join them—to show a point of view from within the psychiatric community.

She was able to find someone, but he was unwilling to appear in front of the panel without hiding his face behind a mask. That masked man became known as Dr. H. Anonymous. He was later revealed to be Philadelphia psychiatrist John E. Fryer. He told the panel he was fearful of revealing his sexuality in his own profession. The panel helped convince the APA to remove homosexuality from its list of mental illnesses in 1973.

Republican presidential candidate Barry Goldwater. In 1972, he moved to San Francisco, where he got involved in the gay rights movement. Five years later, and after several failed campaigns, the openly gay Milk was elected to the San Francisco Board of Supervisors. A gifted speaker, he was able to electrify crowds, both gay and straight. Along with San Francisco mayor George Moscone, he worked to pass gay-friendly measures, such as a 1978 gay rights city ordinance that protected gays from being fired from their jobs.

San Francisco had one of the most visible gay populations in the country at the time, and the city tended to support gay rights issues. Still, not every member of the board of supervisors was supportive. Board member Dan White adamantly voted against the gay rights ordinance. When it passed, he abruptly resigned from the board. Soon afterward, he had a change of heart and tried to convince Moscone to reinstate him. Milk argued against it. He considered White mentally unstable and did not want him back on the board. The mayor agreed.

On the morning of November 27, 1978, White entered San Francisco's City Hall through a basement window. He went upstairs to Moscone's office and shot him. Then he walked to Milk's office and shot him. Both men died from their wounds.

VOICES OF THE MOVEMENT

In a speech on March 10, 1978, Harvey Milk spoke about how his actions—and others'—can give hope to all of those in the gay community:

"The only thing they have to look forward to is hope. And you have to give them hope. . . . Hope that all will be all right. Without hope, not only gays, but the blacks, the seniors, the handicapped . . . will give up. . . .

So if there is a message I have to give, it is that if I've found one overriding thing about my personal election, it's the fact that if a gay person can be elected, it's a green light. And you and you and you, you have to give people hope." [5]

Harvey Milk became a legend in the gay rights movement after his murder in 1978.

That night, thousands of mourners gathered for a candlelight vigil to honor the slain men.[6] Every year since then, people have gathered at the corner of San Francisco's Castro and Market Streets (now called Harvey Milk Plaza) to commemorate the anniversary of their deaths. "Harvey Milk was a visionary whose life and death had a profound effect on the lesbian, gay, bisexual, transgender community. He is remembered for his passion and his perseverance in his quest for equality for all people," his former aide, Anne Kronenberg, said at the 2012 vigil.[7]

ANITA BRYANT AND THE CHALLENGE FROM THE RIGHT

In the 1970s, gays and lesbians were winning important positions in government. They were successfully lobbying for antidiscrimination laws in cities such as Ann Arbor, Michigan; Seattle, Washington; and Saint Paul, Minnesota. Yet it was very clear the struggle for gay rights was far from over. Many people still vehemently opposed gay rights. The biggest foes in the 1970s were certain religious conservatives.

Anita Bryant was one of the most outspoken antigay conservatives. She was a singer, a former Miss Oklahoma beauty queen, and a Florida orange juice spokesperson. In January 1977, the Dade County, Florida, Board of Commissioners voted to end discrimination against gays in housing and employment. Bryant felt homosexuality was wrong, and she did not think the government should support gay rights. She launched a campaign called Save Our Children to fight the Dade County commission's decision and convince voters in Florida that gay people were immoral.

Bryant was able to collect 65,000 signatures in favor of a referendum—a chance for Dade County residents to vote on the issue.[8] On June 7, 1977, they did vote, and they repealed the ordinance by a two-to-one margin. Between 1977 and 1980, Bryant's campaign also helped overturn gay rights bills in places such as Wichita, Kansas, and Eugene, Oregon. The campaign overturned Saint Paul antidiscrimination laws gay activists had helped pass a few years earlier.

A year later in California, state senator John Briggs launched his own antigay effort. His goal was to pass an initiative called Proposition 6 or the Briggs Initiative. The law would prevent gay people from teaching in public schools and fire "notorious homosexuals" from any jobs in direct contact with children.[9]

Fighting the opposition galvanized the gay rights groups and won their cause some much-needed publicity. For the first time, the words *gay* and *homosexual* appeared in newspapers and were spoken on TV and radio stations across the country. The flurry of media attention made gay rights a major topic

PIE IN THE FACE

In 1977, Bryant was discussing the recent success of her national antigay campaign at a press conference when four gay activists burst into the room and hurled a pie straight at her shocked face. "Well, at least it's a fruit pie," she responded, as filling and crust ran down her cheeks.[10] Her comment was a reference to *fruit*, a derogatory term for gay people.

It was one of the first times activists had tried to humiliate a public figure by throwing a pie at his or her face. Since then, various activist groups with various campaigns have "pied" famous faces, including Microsoft founder Bill Gates and former Enron CEO Jeffrey Skilling.

of conversation across the country. In its countercampaign, the gay community recruited some well-respected gay spokespeople, including former NFL player David Kopay and Vietnam War veteran Leonard Matlovich, to speak out against the antigay movement.

Ultimately, California voters struck down Proposition 6. And in 1978, voters in Madison, Wisconsin, also said no when local conservative ministers tried to abolish that city's equal opportunities ordinance. Other cities, such as Seattle, Washington, also rejected attempts to repeal antidiscrimination laws. Gay rights activists had fought back—and won.

FIRST MARCH ON WASHINGTON

Angered by the murders of Milk and Moscone in San Francisco and empowered by their victories against conservative Christians, the gay community came together for a show of unity on October 14, 1979. At least 100,000 demonstrators marched proudly down Pennsylvania Avenue in Washington, DC, for the first National March on Washington for Lesbian and Gay Rights.[11] The march was patterned in the tradition of the 1963 March on Washington for Jobs and Freedom, led by civil rights leaders including Martin Luther King Jr.

The march came ten years after Stonewall and almost a year after the murders. It helped transform

the scattering of gay rights groups around the country into an organized, unified, and proud movement. The *San Francisco Chronicle* called the march the "coming out of the movement on the national political agenda."[12] By 1987, the annual march included as many as 1 million people.[13] ●

CHAPTER 7

GAY RIGHTS IN THE TIME OF AIDS

As the 1980s dawned, the gay rights movement was making strides toward equality and fighting back against opposition. But they were about to be challenged by a foe no one could have foreseen.

On July 3, 1981, the *New York Times* ran a story headlined, "Rare Cancer Seen in 41 Homosexuals."

The article was about an outbreak of Kaposi's sarcoma, a
very rare cancer that had in the past appeared only in older
Italian and Jewish men. Suddenly, Kaposi's was striking
young men. The men had only one thing in common: they
were all gay.

The strange disease causing Kaposi's sarcoma in
these men soon had a name: acquired immune deficiency
syndrome (AIDS). In 1983, researchers in France
discovered that the human immunodeficiency virus (HIV)
causes AIDS. They found it was transmitted through
bodily fluids. One of the ways people could acquire HIV
was through sexual intercourse, both homosexual and
heterosexual, with an infected partner.

AIDS came to define gay America by the mid-1980s, as
thousands of gay men died from the disease. Because there
was so much fear and misinformation regarding AIDS
transmission, many people who became sick were harassed
or shunned. Many were evicted from their homes, fired
from their jobs, or refused insurance coverage. Some
religious conservatives claimed AIDS was a "plague" sent
to punish gay people.[1] Reverend Jerry Falwell stated,
"AIDS is the wrath of God upon homosexuals."[2] The US
government, under President Ronald Reagan, did not
respond quickly to the health crisis. President Reagan did

PRESIDENT REAGAN AND AIDS

President Ronald Reagan is considered an icon among conservative politicians. Yet among people at the center of the AIDS crisis, his legacy is far less positive. Reagan did not publically address AIDS until May 31, 1987, at a Washington, DC, conference. By that time, more than 36,000 Americans had already been diagnosed and almost 21,000 had died from the disease.[3]

Reagan was supported in large part by religious conservatives and a political group called the Moral Majority, which was founded by Reverend Falwell. Such groups did not support spending government money on AIDS research.

But the next president, George H. W. Bush, also a Republican, signed two important pieces of AIDS legislation. The Americans with Disabilities Act of 1990 provided equal opportunities for people with AIDS in housing, employment, transportation, and other services. And the Ryan White Comprehensive AIDS Resources Emergency (CARE) Act of 1990 set aside millions of dollars for AIDS-related services for patients and their families.

not talk publicly about AIDS until very late in his presidency.

BANDING TOGETHER TO FIGHT AIDS

In response to what they saw as a lack of action by the US government, gay rights activists began mobilizing. They formed groups such as the AIDS Coalition to Unleash Power (ACT UP) and Queer Nation. They held marches, including a 1984 demonstration at the Democratic National Convention in San Francisco. Activist Cleve Jones created the AIDS Memorial Quilt to commemorate the thousands of people—gay and straight—who had died from the disease.

Activist groups demanded more money to fund research for AIDS. They wanted to stop discrimination against people with the disease. And they asked for the same basic rights straight, married couples had long taken for granted. This included the right for one partner to visit the other in the hospital and the right to inherit money and property from a partner who died.

These groups had to overcome many stereotypes about AIDS. They had to convince frightened people they could not acquire AIDS through casual contact

AIDS MEMORIAL QUILT

By the mid-1980s, thousands of gay men—as well as numerous straight people—had contracted AIDS. San Francisco gay rights activist Cleve Jones decided to create a memorial. In 1985, he asked supporters to write on cards the names of their loved ones who had died of AIDS. When those cards were taped to the wall of the San Francisco Federal Building, they looked like a patchwork quilt.

Jones decided to create a real, bigger quilt to honor AIDS victims. The first panel was dedicated to Marvin Feldman, his friend who had died from AIDS. People began sending in panels from around the country. On October 11, 1987, the quilt was displayed for the first time in Washington, DC, during the National March on Washington for Lesbian and Gay Rights. It included almost 2,000 panels and was larger than a football field.[4] By 2012, the AIDS Memorial Quilt included more than 48,000 panels and covered 1.3 million square feet (121,000 sq m).[5]

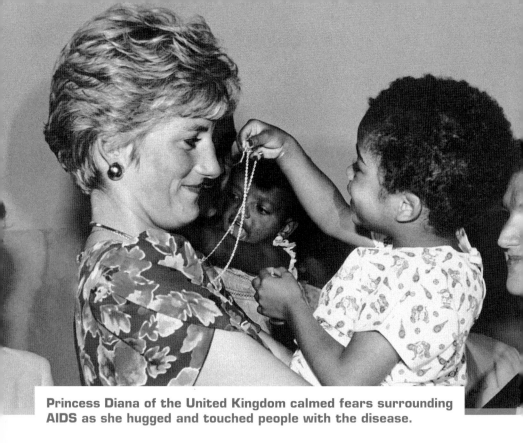

Princess Diana of the United Kingdom calmed fears surrounding AIDS as she hugged and touched people with the disease.

with someone infected with the disease—for example, by hugging or using the same toilet. Celebrities helped erase some of the stigma from the disease. Actor Rock Hudson revealed he had AIDS in July 1985, three months before he died. Princess Diana was filmed and photographed many times hugging AIDS patients.

BATTLING ANTIGAY LAWS

Not only was AIDS considered a menace in the 1980s, but sexual intercourse between gay couples came under fire again, too. Gay men and women could be arrested in their own homes for being intimate with the person they loved.

In August 1982, police burst into the Atlanta, Georgia, home of Michael Hardwick because he had failed to appear in court on a public drinking charge. When they opened the door to his bedroom, they found him in bed with another man. The police promptly arrested Hardwick under Georgia's antisodomy laws. Hardwick sued the state of Georgia, claiming the arrest violated his constitutional rights. By a five-to-four vote, the US Supreme Court ruled against him in June 1986. The justices argued the US Constitution does not protect sexual relations between gay people.

Yet the issue was far from over. On October 14, 1987, a group of approximately 2,000 people protested the Hardwick decision outside the Supreme Court Building in Washington, DC.[6] At least 600 of them were arrested.[7]

NATIONAL COMING OUT DAY

For years, many gay people were afraid to "come out" for fear they would be shunned from their families and fired from their jobs. But in 1988, a group of gay activists decided it was time to not only accept the idea of coming out, but to embrace it and encourage it.

Their idea was to host a National Coming Out Day every October 11—the anniversary of the 1987 National March on Washington for Lesbian and Gay Rights. The annual event is meant to encourage gay people to live openly and be proud of who they are. Since then, every year's event has had a different theme, such as "Coming Out for Equality" or "It's a Family Affair."[8]

The 1980s AIDS epidemic posed a challenge on both a personal and political level for the gay rights movement. But it also ignited supporters to keep moving forward in their quest. ●

**Activists observe a moment of silence near »
the AIDS Quilt as it is displayed for the first
time in Washington, DC, in 1987.**

CHAPTER 8

SEARCHING FOR A VOICE

For much of the 1900s, gay people had a very hard time finding role models, even in the media. In the early days of television, it was rare to see an openly gay character. When gay characters did appear on television, they were usually portrayed negatively—such as the violent lesbian women who killed retirement-home residents for their money in a 1974 episode of the *Police Woman* series. The first recurring gay character in a series was Jodie Dallas, played by Billy Crystal, on the late 1970s sitcom *Soap*. Yet gay rights groups saw his character as a negative stereotype.

In November 1985, the Gay and Lesbian Alliance Against Defamation worked to get more accurate portrayals of gay people in television and the movies. Still, it took another decade for gay people to become regular—and positively portrayed—characters. Ellen DeGeneres is credited with opening up prime-time television to gay actors and characters when she came out on a 1997 episode of her sitcom, *Ellen*. While supporters championed her decision, it also caused a swift backlash. Many advertisers, including fast-food restaurant Wendy's and

CELEBRITIES COMING OUT

For years, most gay celebrities remained deeply closeted. It was not until the 1970s that celebrities started coming out of the closet. In 1975, former NFL running back David Kopay became the first professional athlete to come out. He was followed by tennis players Billie Jean King and Martina Navratilova in 1981. By the early 2000s, more and more famous people were proudly out of the closet, including actress Rosie O'Donnell and singer George Michael. In the years that followed, celebrities such as actor Neil Patrick Harris, news anchor Anderson Cooper, and actress Jodie Foster came out as well. In 2013, basketball player Jason Collins became the first athlete to come out while still playing in one of the major sports leagues.

car manufacturer Chrysler, backed out of buying airtime on the show. Some local ABC networks refused to air the episode.

Nevertheless, *Ellen* was able to break new ground. By the early 2000s, shows such as *The L Word*, *Will and Grace*, and *Queer Eye for the Straight Guy* were part of the television lineup. In 2012, almost 5 percent of all television characters on the major networks were gay, bisexual, or transgender.[1]

DON'T ASK, DON'T TELL

As gay characters began to be represented on television, gay people were also fighting for their right to be represented in the military. For most of the 1900s, the US military forbade homosexual and heterosexual sodomy under the Uniform Code of Military Justice, but it did not prohibit gay people from serving. Gay people were often given noncombat roles. Many chose not to reveal their sexuality.

But then in 1981, the Department of Defense created a uniform policy across all branches of the military. It introduced a directive that stated, "Homosexuality is incompatible with military service."[2] This meant military members could be discharged just for being gay. Starting in 1982, all new recruits had to reveal their sexual orientation when they enlisted.

When Bill Clinton was running for president in 1992, one of his campaign promises was to lift the ban on gays in the military. In 1993, as president, Clinton tried to change the policy. He said at the time,

The issue is whether men and women who can and have served with real distinction should be excluded from military service solely on the basis of their status. And I believe they should not.[3]

The move faced fierce opposition, especially from antigay groups and Georgia senator Sam Nunn, chair of the Senate Armed Services Committee. Clinton eventually settled on a compromise. Called "Don't Ask, Don't Tell," the policy allowed gays to serve

SERVING IN SILENCE

Norwegian-born Margarethe Cammermeyer joined the US military in 1961 as an army nurse. She served in Germany and then Vietnam before moving to Seattle and joining the US Army Reserve. In the late 1980s, as a high-ranking colonel, Cammermeyer identified herself as a lesbian. During an interview for security clearance in 1989, she revealed her sexual orientation to the military.

Cammermeyer's revelation resulted in her being expelled from the military. She hired an attorney and challenged the ban on gays in the military. She and her lawyer spent several years in court arguing for her right to serve.

In June 1994, Cammermeyer was reinstated to her past position of chief nurse in the US National Guard. She retired in 1997 after more than 30 years of military service.

Gay rights groups were outraged when Clinton signed "Don't Ask, Don't Tell" into law.

in the military as long as they did not reveal their sexual orientation or engage in same-sex acts. It was signed into law in October 1993. To gay groups, Clinton's signing of "Don't Ask, Don't Tell" was a huge loss.

SAME-SEX MARRIAGE AND CIVIL UNIONS

As early as the 1970s, same-sex couples were asserting their rights to get married legally and were challenging the ban on same-sex marriage. Gay couples wanted the same rights straight couples received through marriage, such as employee benefits, Social Security payments to spouses, and visitation rights to children in the case of a breakup.

In 1970, Jack Baker and James Michael McConnell applied for a marriage license in Minneapolis, Minnesota. A year later, gay activists Paul Barwick and John Singer applied for a marriage license in Seattle, Washington. Both couples were refused. The Washington court responded by saying, "It was as preposterous for a man to argue that he had a right to marry a man as it would be for a man to argue that he had a right to get pregnant."[4] Singer and McConnell lost their jobs. However, these couples, along with the few other gay couples who attempted to marry at that time, did draw attention to the issue of gay marriage.

In the 1970s, groups in several states—including Minnesota, Washington, and Kentucky—legally challenged same-sex marriage bans. They argued that prohibiting gay marriage went against the US Constitution, which legally protects the rights of all American citizens. The courts rejected their claims.

Then in 1990, three gay couples applied for marriage licenses in Hawaii and were turned down. They filed a lawsuit against the state. In a landmark decision, the Supreme Court of Hawaii ruled that allowing only straight couples to get married violated the state's constitution and discriminated on the basis of gender. It was the first time a court had suggested same-sex couples had the right to marry, and the case inspired couples in other states to also file lawsuits.

But conservative groups fought back. In March 1995, Utah governor Mike Leavitt signed the nation's first "defense of marriage" law preventing the recognition of same-sex marriage. A number of states followed suit, adding laws and amendments to their constitutions defining marriage specifically as between a man and a woman.

On September 21, 1996, Clinton signed the Defense of Marriage Act (DOMA), which denied

BAKER AND MCCONNELL

On May 18, 1970, Baker and McConnell became the first gay couple to request a legal marriage. They invited reporters to come with them as they went to the Hennepin County, Minnesota, clerk's office to request the marriage license. The clerk refused. The couple appealed to the Minnesota Supreme Court, but their argument was rejected.

In August 1971, McConnell legally adopted Baker. Adoption was the only way gay partners could have legal rights with each other. Baker took the name Pat Lynn McConnell. Because it sounded like a woman's name, the pair was able to get a marriage license from Blue Earth County, Minnesota. They were married in Minneapolis on September 3, 1971.

Although the county attorney eventually declared the marriage void, it was still considered a victory. The media attention allowed the public to see a gay couple in a loving, committed relationship.

same-sex couples federal marriage rights. It also allowed states to not recognize gay marriages that had been performed in other states. DOMA was a huge blow to the gay rights movement.

THE FIGHT FOR FAMILY RIGHTS

Gay people were not only fighting for equality in their relationships. They were also fighting for access to their own children. In the 1970s and 1980s, most courts ruled against gay parents in custody cases. That meant any gay or lesbian parent who had been in a heterosexual marriage and went through a divorce could lose custody of his or her children to the other, straight parent. Many states also restricted gay couples from adopting or becoming foster parents. These decisions were driven by fears that gay parents would raise their children to be gay or that the children might be stigmatized because of their parents' sexual orientation.

Yet when researchers began studying the children of gay and lesbian parents, they did not find any evidence they were more likely to be gay themselves or have any extra emotional problems. In fact, the evidence showed children raised by gay parents were as well-adjusted as children raised by straight parents. A 1995 review of research by the American Psychological Association concluded, "Not a single study has found children of gay and lesbian parents to be disadvantaged in any significant respect relative to children of heterosexual parents."[5] Despite these findings, progress on rights for gay parents was very slow as the gay rights movement prepared to enter a new millennium. ●

CHAPTER 9

A NEW ERA IN GAY RIGHTS

By the start of the 2000s, the gay rights movement had made significant gains. Many gay people chose to come out. They finally had role models to respect and emulate in entertainment, sports, and politics. They were gaining ground on the major issues, from same-sex marriage to discrimination in employment. Yet they had not achieved full equality yet.

MARRIAGE EQUALITY

By the early 2000s, some cities and states considered offering benefits to same-sex couples through legally recognized domestic partnerships or civil unions. These labels gave both gay and straight couples many—but not all—of the legal benefits of marriage. In 2000, Vermont became the first state to legally recognize same-sex civil unions.

In November 2003, the Massachusetts Supreme Court ruled in a lawsuit that denying marriage rights to gays violated the state's constitution. During a constitutional

RELATIONSHIP RIGHTS

On November 13, 1983, an accident left Sharon Kowalski brain damaged and physically disabled. Kowalski's partner of four years, Karen Thompson, rushed to the hospital. Although the two women considered themselves married, Thompson had no legal rights. She could not make any medical decisions. Those decisions were left to Kowalski's parents. They took Kowalski to their home and forbade Thompson from seeing their daughter.

Thompson embarked on a prolonged legal battle to be reunited with her partner and make medical decisions on her behalf. Gay and lesbian advocates around the country joined the fight. On February 2, 1989, Thompson finally won, and she and Kowalski were reunited.

A 2011 federal regulation now prohibits most hospitals from denying visitation rights based on sexual orientation.

convention, President George W. Bush and Massachusetts governor Mitt Romney tried to encourage the legislature to change the constitution to deny the ruling. But on May 17, 2004, Massachusetts began issuing marriage licenses to gay and lesbian couples. When Marcia Hams and Susan Shepherd wed at the city hall in Cambridge, Massachusetts, they became the first same-sex couple in the United States to be legally married.

Yet even as state supreme courts were sanctioning gay marriage across the country, citizens in some states were voting it down. On May 15, 2008, the California Supreme Court ruled gay people had the constitutional right to get married. Between May and November of that year, more than 18,000 same-sex couples were married.[1] Then in November, California voters approved Proposition 8, a measure banning same-sex marriages. But on February 7, 2012, a federal appeals court struck down Proposition 8. This ruling cleared the way for the US Supreme Court to rule on Proposition 8 in June 2013. That same month, the court was also set to rule on whether the national Defense of Marriage Act was constitutional.

As of spring 2013, Washington, DC, and 12 states—Connecticut, Delaware, Iowa, Maine, Maryland, Massachusetts, Minnesota, New Hampshire, New York, Rhode Island, Vermont, and Washington—had legalized gay marriage.[2] Thirty states had constitutional amendments banning gay marriage, and six states had laws banning gay marriage.[3]

PRESIDENTS AND GAY RIGHTS

The gay rights movement has seen varied amounts of presidential support. After Reagan, George H. W. Bush signed AIDS legislation in the early 1990s. After Bush, Clinton's attempt to reverse the ban on gays serving in the military resulted in the "Don't Ask, Don't Tell" policy. He also signed the Defense of Marriage Act, which bans the national government from recognizing same-sex marriages, even though it does allow the states to recognize same-sex marriage. However, he achieved a few victories for gay rights. Clinton signed executive orders allowing security clearance for gay people and prohibiting antigay discrimination in the federal civilian workforce.

MAYOR NEWSOM AND GAY MARRIAGE IN SAN FRANCISCO

On February 12, 2004, San Francisco mayor Gavin Newsom took a bold step. Against his state's laws, he ordered his city's clerk to issue marriage licenses to same-sex couples. "I do not believe it's appropriate for me, as mayor of San Francisco, to discriminate against people," he said, defending his decision. "And if that means my political career ends, so be it."[4]

Newsom's career did not end, but the California Supreme Court ruled the estimated 4,000 same-sex marriages that were held in San Francisco invalid.[5]

He also lobbied for passage of the Employment Non-Discrimination Act, prohibiting job discrimination based on sexual orientation. Before he left office, Clinton also signed a proclamation making June National Gay and Lesbian Pride Month. He also appointed more openly gay and lesbian officials than any president before him.

As a Republican supported by conservative Christians, George W. Bush did not endorse any gay rights legislation. But at the same time, he did not repeal any legislation Clinton had passed. George W. Bush was also the first Republican president to appoint an openly gay man to serve in his administration, making Scott Evertz the director of the Office of National AIDS Policy. During George W. Bush's presidency, the Supreme Court ruled in the *Lawrence v. Texas* case on June 26, 2003. The decision states that the Constitution does protect sexual contact between any consenting adults. The ruling overturned all antisodomy laws in the states.

When Obama was elected president, he went even further toward providing gay rights. He signed the hate crimes prevention act into law in 2009. On December 22, 2010, he repealed "Don't Ask, Don't Tell," allowing openly gay people to serve in the military. And on May 9, 2012, during an interview with *ABC News*, Obama said he

**Marchers at a gay pride event in 2008 show support »
for then-presidential candidate Barack Obama.**

supported gay marriage. "It signifies a history-changing moment when a president finally says, 'I'm on your side,'" said Stacy Lentz, co-owner of the Stonewall Inn.[6]

MATTHEW SHEPARD AND THE HATE CRIMES PREVENTION ACT

On October 7, 1998, two men abducted 21-year-old Matthew Shepard, an openly gay man, from a bar and drove him to a remote area near Laramie, Wyoming. After tying him to a fence, the men beat Shepard with the butt of a pistol. Then they left him for dead. Shepard died in a hospital on October 12.

More than a decade later, on October 28, 2009, Obama signed into law a hate crimes prevention act bearing Shepard's name, as well as the name of James Byrd Jr., an African American killed by white supremacists in 1998. The act expands the legal definition of a hate crime by including any crime committed based on a person's sex, sexual orientation, or gender identity a hate crime. Those found guilty of hate crimes face harsher penalties.

THE MOVEMENT KEEPS ON

The fight for gay rights is far from over. People can still be fired in most states for being gay. Gay marriage is illegal in most of the country. People still face discrimination, hatred, and violence because of their sexual orientation. Young gay people often still face discrimination and bullying in schools.

Yet the movement has made undeniable strides since Franklin Kameny took on the Civil Service Commission and patrons of the Stonewall

While serving as a top official in Obama's cabinet, Secretary of State Hillary Clinton addressed the importance of gay rights at a speech to the United Nations on December 6, 2011:

VOICES OF THE MOVEMENT

" Like being a woman, like being a racial, religious, tribal, or ethnic minority, being LGBT does not make you less human. And that is why gay rights are human rights, and human rights are gay rights. . . . It is a violation of human rights when people are beaten or killed because of their sexual orientation, or because they do not conform to cultural norms about how men and women should look or behave. It is a violation of human rights when governments declare it illegal to be gay, or allow those who harm gay people to go unpunished. . . . No matter what we look like, where we come from, or who we are, we are all equally entitled to our human rights and dignity. . . . All people deserve to be treated with dignity and have their human rights respected, no matter who they are or whom they love. " [7]

Inn hurled bottles at raiding police officers. More than half of Americans polled in 2013 said they support gay marriage.[8] This was an increase from 39 percent in 2008.[9] And for the first time, a president has pledged his support for gay rights and gay marriage.

The 2000s have been a time of incredible momentum for the gay, lesbian, bisexual, and transgender community. As advocate Matt Foreman said, "While enormous and heart-wrenching inequities remain, progress over the last ten years has been extraordinary."[10] ●

**Participants at a 2011 gay pride parade celebrate »
the success the movement has achieved.**

TIMELINE

1924
On December 10, Henry Gerber founds the Society for Human Rights.

1951
Harry Hay's Mattachine Society holds its first meeting.

1958
The Supreme Court rules on January 13 that the magazine *One* can be sent through the US Postal Service.

1961
On January 21, Franklin Kameny argues his firing from the Army Map Service before the US Supreme Court.

1969
On June 28, police raid the Stonewall Inn, setting off a riot.

1974
Elaine Noble becomes the first openly gay person to be elected to state government; Congresswoman Bella Abzug introduces the first national gay civil rights bill.

1978
On November 27, Harvey Milk and George Moscone are murdered in San Francisco by former board member Dan White.

1979
The first National March on Washington for Lesbian and Gay Rights is held on October 14.

1981
On July 3, the *New York Times* reports on an outbreak of a rare cancer that is later discovered to be caused by HIV.

1981 The US military declares homosexuality "incompatible with military service."

1993 Bill Clinton signs "Don't Ask, Don't Tell" into law.

1996 Clinton signs the Defense of Marriage Act (DOMA) on September 21.

2000 Vermont becomes the first state to legally recognize same-sex civil unions.

2003 In the case *Lawrence v. Texas*, the US Supreme Court overturns the nation's antisodomy laws on June 26.

2004 On May 17, Massachusetts begins issuing marriage licenses to gay and lesbian couples.

2009 On October 28, Barack Obama signs the hate crimes prevention act into law.

2010 Obama repeals "Don't Ask, Don't Tell" on December 22.

SAME-SEX MARRIAGE IN US STATES: 2013

- Same-sex marriage allowed
- Unions and partnerships allowed
- Same-sex marriage banned
- No provisions on gay marriage

DATE OF THE MOVEMENT'S BEGINNING

1920s

LOCATIONS

Stonewall Inn, Greenwich Village, New York; San Francisco, California; Washington, DC

KEY PLAYERS

Gay rights pioneer **Harry Hay** founded the country's first gay rights organization, the Mattachine Society, in 1951.

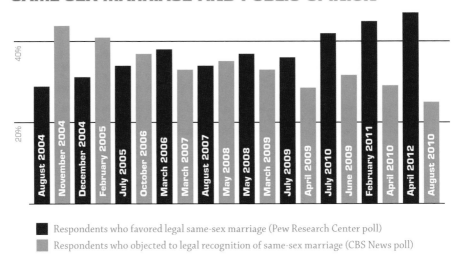

SAME-SEX MARRIAGE AND PUBLIC OPINION

40%

20%

August 2004
November 2004
December 2004
February 2005
July 2005
October 2006
March 2006
March 2007
August 2007
May 2008
May 2008
March 2009
July 2009
April 2009
July 2010
June 2009
February 2011
April 2010
April 2012
August 2010

■ Respondents who favored legal same-sex marriage (Pew Research Center poll)
■ Respondents who objected to legal recognition of same-sex marriage (CBS News poll)

Franklin Kameny was fired from his US government job in 1957 because he was gay. Kameny's case was the first gay rights case to appear before the US Supreme Court. He lost, but he later helped others win similar court battles.

Harvey Milk was an eloquent champion for gay rights in San Francisco. He was murdered on November 27, 1978, and his legacy inspired the gay rights cause.

GOALS AND OUTCOMES

The gay rights movement has worked steadily to increase societal acceptance of homosexuality and extend equal rights to LGBT people, including hospital visitation, adoption, fair housing, employment rights, and freedom from bullying. Discriminatory laws have been struck down in many states, while the fight for gay marriage continues in the 2010s.

GLOSSARY

assimilate
To blend in with social and cultural norms.

conformist
Someone who dresses or acts in a way that is accepted by society.

conservative
A person who has traditional views about politics, religion, and society that he or she does not want to change.

discrimination
Treating a person differently because of the group to which he or she belongs.

flamboyant
Given to elaborate or colorful display or behavior.

galvanize
To excite or cause someone to take action.

heterosexual
Someone who is attracted to people of the opposite sex; straight.

homophile
Relating to people who are attracted to members of their own sex.

immoral
Not following accepted standards of what is right or wrong.

liberal
A person who politically supports social equality.

lobby

To attempt to change a politician's position on an issue.

Mafia

An organized group of criminals.

pervert

Someone who engages in or thinks about engaging in sexual behavior that is not considered normal.

procreation

The act of conceiving a baby.

stigma

Marked by a quality that causes disgrace in other people.

transgender

Someone who identifies with or acts like a different gender than he or she was born.

ADDITIONAL RESOURCES

SELECTED BIBLIOGRAPHY

Biagi, Shirley and Marilyn Kern-Foxworth. *Facing Difference: Race, Gender, and Mass Media*. Thousand Oaks, CA: Pine Forge, 1997. Print.

Marcus, Eric. *Making Gay History: The Half-Century Fight for Lesbian and Gay Equal Rights*. New York: HarperCollins, 2002. Print.

Morris, Bonnie J. "History of Lesbian, Gay, & Bisexual Social Movements." *American Psychological Association*. American Psychological Association, n.d. Web. 22 Feb. 2013.

Murdoch, Joyce and Deb Price. *Courting Justice: Gay Men and Lesbians v. the Supreme Court*. New York: Basic, 2001. Print.

Shilts, Randy. *The Mayor of Castro Street: The Life and Times of Harvey Milk*. New York: Macmillan, 2008. Print.

FURTHER READINGS

Alsenas, Linas. *Gay America: Struggle for Equality*. New York: Amulet, 2008. Print.

Burns, Kate. *Gay Rights Activists*. Farmington Hills, MI: Lucent, 2005. Print.

Marcus, Eric. *What If Someone I Know Is Gay? Answers to Questions About What It Means to Be Gay and Lesbian*. New York: Simon Pulse, 2007. Print.

WEB SITES

To learn more about the gay rights movement, visit ABDO
Publishing Company online at **www.abdopublishing.com**.
Web sites about the gay rights movement are featured on our
Book Links page. These links are routinely monitored and
updated to provide the most current information available.

PLACES TO VISIT

The AIDS Memorial Quilt

204 Fourteenth Street NW
Atlanta, Georgia 30318
404-688-5500
http://www.aidsquilt.org
The AIDS Memorial Quilt travels on exhibit around the
country. Visit the AIDS Memorial Quilt Web site for
information on upcoming shows.

GLBT History Museum

4127 Eighteenth Street
San Francisco, CA 94114
415-621-1107
http://www.glbthistory.org/museum/index.html
The museum explores the history of San Francisco's GLBT
community.

Harvey Milk Plaza

Corner of Castro and Market Streets
San Francisco, CA 94114
The site of the yearly memorial of Harvey Milk and George
Moscone's murders, the location includes a gay pride flag and
a plaque to honor Milk.

SOURCE NOTES

CHAPTER 1. STONEWALL

1. Lionel Wright. "The Stonewall Riots–1969–A Turning Point in the Struggle for Gay and Lesbian Liberation." *SocialistAlternative.org*. Socialist Alternative, 1 July 1999. Web. 8 Apr. 2013.

2. Marcus, Eric. *Making Gay History: The Half-Century Fight for Lesbian and Gay Equal Rights*. New York: HarperCollins, 2002. Print. 127.

3. "Stonewall at 40: The *Voice* Articles That Sparked a Final Night of Rioting." *Village Voice*. Village Voice, 24 June 2009. Web. 8 Apr. 2013.

4. David Carter. *Stonewall: The Riots That Sparked the Gay Revolution*. New York: Macmillan, 2010. Print. 164.

5. Various. "Stonewall at 40: The *Voice* Articles That Sparked a Final Night of Rioting." *Village Voice*. Village Voice, 24 June 2009. Web. 8 Apr. 2013.

6. David Carter. *Stonewall: The Riots That Sparked the Gay Revolution*. New York: Macmillan, 2010. Print. 204.

7. Jerry Lisker. "Homo Nest Raided, Queen Bees Are Stinging Mad: *The New York Daily News*. 6 July 1969." *American Experience*. WGBH Educational Foundation, n.d. Web. 8 Apr. 2013.

8. Ibid.

9. David Carter. *Stonewall: The Riots That Sparked the Gay Revolution*. New York: Macmillan, 2010. Print. 189.

10. Ibid. 302.

11. Simon Hall. *American Patriotism, American Protest: Social Movements Since the Sixties*. Philadelphia: University of Pennsylvania, 2010. Print. 33.

CHAPTER 2. A TIME OF DARKNESS

1. Plato. *The Symposium of Plato*. Boston: Branden, 1996. Print. 6.

2. Susan E. Henking. *Que(e)rying Religion: A Critical Anthology*. London: Continuum International, 1997. Print. 40.

3. John D. Bessler. *Cruel and Unusual: The American Death Penalty and the Founders' Eighth Amendment*. Lebanon, NH: Northeastern UP, 2012. Print. 143.

4. Salvatore J. Licata and Robert P. Petersen, ed. *Historical Perspectives on Homosexuality: The Gay Past: A Collection of Historical Essays*. New York: Psychology Press/ Hawthorne, 1981. Print. 20.

5. Joseph Bristow. *Oscar Wilde and Modern Culture: The Making of a Legend*. Athens, OH: Ohio UP, 2008. Print. 244.

6. "Just the Facts about Sexual Orientation and Youth." *American Psychological Association*. American Psychological Association, 2008. Web. 28 Apr. 2013.

7. Peter Gay. *Freud: A Life for Our Time*. New York: Norton, 1998. Print. 610.

8. "Nazi Persecution of Homosexuals 1933–1945." *United States Holocaust Memorial Museum*. United States Holocaust Memorial Museum, n.d. Web. 28 Apr. 2013.

9. "Prevalence of Homosexuality." *Kinsey Institute*. Kinsey Institute for Research in Sex, Gender, and Reproduction, n.d. Web. 28 Apr. 2013.

10. Vern L. Bullough. *Before Stonewall: Activists for Gay and Lesbian Rights in Historical Context*. Oxford, UK: Psychology, 2002. Print. 25.

CHAPTER 3. THE HOMOPHILE MOVEMENT

1. Associated Press. "Supreme Court Strikes Down Texas Law Banning Sodomy." *New York Times*. New York Times, 26 June 2003. Web. 28 Apr. 2013.

2. Joyce Murdoch and Deb Price. *Courting Justice: Gay Men and Lesbians v. the Supreme Court*. New York: Basic, 2001. Print. 37.

3. Jennifer Terry. *An American Obsession: Science, Medicine, and Homosexuality in Modern Society*. Chicago: U of Chicago, 1999. Print. 271.

4. Joyce Murdoch and Deb Price. *Courting Justice: Gay Men and Lesbians v. the Supreme Court*. New York: Basic, 2001. Print. 38.

5. Susan Donaldson James. "Lavender Scare: U.S. Fired 5,000 Gays in 1953 'Witch Hunt.'" *ABC Good Morning America*. Yahoo! ABC News Network, 5 Mar. 2012. Web. 28 Apr. 2013.

6. Eric Marcus. *Making Gay History: The Half-Century Fight for Lesbian and Gay Equal Rights*. New York: HarperCollins, 2002. Print. 40.

7. Ibid.

8. Ibid.

9. Joyce Murdoch and Deb Price. *Courting Justice: Gay Men and Lesbians v. the Supreme Court*. New York: Basic, 2001. Print. 27.

10. Ibid. 27.

11. John D'Emilio, William B. Turner, Urvashi Vaid, ed. *Creating Change: Sexuality, Public Policy, and Civil Rights*. New York: St. Martin's, 2000. Print. 162.

12. Joyce Murdoch and Deb Price. *Courting Justice: Gay Men and Lesbians v. the Supreme Court*. New York: Basic, 2001. Print. 28.

CHAPTER 4. THE FIRST FIGHT BACK

1. Susan Donaldson James. "Lavender Scare: U.S. Fired 5,000 Gays in 1953 'Witch Hunt.'" *ABC Good Morning America*. Yahoo! ABC News Network, 5 Mar. 2012. Web. 28 Apr. 2013.

2. "The Lavender Scare—Trailer." *YouTube*. YouTube, n.d. Web. 28 Apr. 2013.

3. John D'Emilio, William B. Turner, Urvashi Vaid, ed. *Creating Change: Sexuality, Public Policy, and Civil Rights*. New York: St. Martin's, 2000. Print. 191.

4. Joyce Murdoch and Deb Price. *Courting Justice: Gay Men and Lesbians v. the Supreme Court*. New York: Basic, 2001. Print. 55.

5. "Library of Congress Exhibits Gay Rights History." *Washington Post*. Washington Post, 9 May 2011. Web. 28 Apr. 2013.

6. Jeff Kisseloff. *Generation on Fire: Voices of Protest from the 1960s, An Oral History*. Lexington, KY: UP of Kentucky, 2007. Print. 192.

7. John D'Emilio, William B. Turner, Urvashi Vaid, ed. *Creating Change: Sexuality, Public Policy, and Civil Rights*. New York: St. Martin's, 2000. Print. 155.

8. "APNewsBreak: Gay Rights Papers Shown at US Library." *Kameny Papers*. Kameny Papers, 8 May 2011. Web. 28 Apr. 2013.

9. Ibid.

10. Susan Gluck Mezey. *Queers in Court: Gay Rights Law and Public Policy*. Print. Lanham, MD: Rowman, 2007. Print. 195.

11. Simon Hall. *American Patriotism, American Protest: Social Movements Since the Sixties*. Philadelphia: U of Pennsylvania, 2010. Print. 29.

12. "Gay Pioneers." *YouTube*. YouTube, 29 Dec 2011. Web. 28 Apr. 2013.

13. Simon Hall. *American Patriotism, American Protest: Social Movements Since the Sixties*. Philadelphia: U of Pennsylvania, 2010. Print. 32.

14. John D'Emilio. *Sexual Politics, Sexual Communities: Second Edition*. Chicago: U of Chicago, 1983. Print. 197.

15. Ibid. 199.

16. Kenji Yoshino. *Covering: The Hidden Assault on Our Civil Rights*. New York: Random, 2006. Print. 60.

CHAPTER 5. LAUNCH OF THE GAY RIGHTS MOVEMENT

1. Fred Sargeant. "1970: A First-Person Account of the First Gay Pride March." *Village Voice News*. Village Voice, 22 June 2010. Web. 28 Apr. 2013.

2. Simon Hall. *American Patriotism, American Protest: Social Movements Since the Sixties*. Philadelphia: U of Pennsylvania, 2010. Print. 36.

3. "Biography: Stonewall Participants." *American Experience*. WGBH Educational Foundation, n.d. Web. 8 Apr. 2013.

4. Simon Hall. *American Patriotism, American Protest: Social Movements Since the Sixties*. Philadelphia: U of Pennsylvania, 2010. Print. 37.

5. Elizabeth A. Armstrong. *Forging Gay Identities: Organizing Sexuality in San Francisco, 1950–1994*. Chicago: U of Chicago, 2002. Print. 74.

6. Tom Owens. "One Mother's Voice: PFLAG Cofounder Recalls Group's Beginnings." *PFLAG*. PFLAG, 14 July 2005. Web. 8 Apr. 2013.

7. Ibid.

8. Fred Kuhr. "Family Boosters." *Advocate.com*. Here Media, 30 Aug. 2005. Web. 28 Apr. 2013.

9. "Frequently Asked Questions." PFLAG. PFLAG, n.d. Web. 28 Apr. 2013.

10. Simon Hall. *American Patriotism, American Protest: Social Movements Since the Sixties*. Philadelphia: U of Pennsylvania, 2010. Print. 38.

CHAPTER 6. GOING MAINSTREAM

1. Laura Shapiro. "Elaine Noble: Win, Place or Show?" *Mother Jones* Aug. 1978: 14. Print.

2. Laura Mansnerus. "Bella Abzug, 77, Congresswoman and a Founding Feminist, Is Dead." *New York Times*. New York Times, 1 Apr. 1998. Web. 28 Apr. 2013.

3. Edward Alwood. *Straight News: Gays, Lesbians, and the News Media*. New York: Columbia UP, 1996. Print. 126.

4. Joyce Murdoch and Deb Price. *Courting Justice: Gay Men and Lesbians v. the Supreme Court*. New York: Basic, 2001. Print. 62.

5. Lucas Grindley. "How The Harvey Milk 'Hope Speech' Still Resonates This National Coming Out Day." *Advocate.com*. Here Media, 11 Oct. 2012. Web. 28 Apr. 2013.

6. "Harvey Milk—Biography." Milk Foundation.org. Harvey Milk Foundation, n.d. Web. 28 Apr. 2013.

7. Erin Sherbert. "Remembering Harvey Milk and George Moscone." *SF Weekly*. SF Weekly, 27 Nov. 2012. Web. 28 Apr. 2013.

8. Randy Shilts. *The Mayor of Castro Street: The Life and Times of Harvey Milk*. New York: Macmillan, 2008. Print. 156.

9. John D'Emilio. *Sexual Politics, Sexual Communities: Second Edition*. Chicago: U of Chicago, 1983. Print. 13.

10. "Anita Bryant Pie in the Face." *YouTube*. YouTube. n.d. Web. 28 Apr. 2013.

11. Elizabeth A. Armstrong. *Forging Gay Identities: Organizing Sexuality in San Francisco, 1950–1994*. Chicago: U of Chicago, 2002. Print. 130.

12. Ibid.

13. Bonnie J. Morris. "History of Lesbian, Gay, & Bisexual Social Movements." *American Psychological Association*. American Psychological Association, n.d. Web. 28 Apr. 2013.

CHAPTER 7. GAY RIGHTS IN THE TIME OF AIDS

1. John D'Emilio. *Sexual Politics, Sexual Communities: Second Edition*. Chicago: U of Chicago, 1983. Print. 17.

2. Allen White. "Reagan's AIDS Legacy/Silence Equals Death." *SFGate*. Hearst Communications, 8 June 2004. Web. 28 Apr. 2013.

3. Ibid.

4. "About the AIDS Memorial Quilt." *AIDS Memorial Quilt*. The NAMES Project Foundation, n .d. Web. 28 Apr. 2013.

5. Ibid.

6. John D'Emilio. *Sexual Politics, Sexual Communities*. Chicago: U of Chicago, 1983. Print. 448.

7. Ibid.

8. "The History of Coming Out." *Human Rights Campaign*. Human Rights Campaign, n.d. Web. 28 Apr. 2013.

CHAPTER 8. SEARCHING FOR A VOICE

1. Frazier Moore. "GLAAD's 'Where We Are on TV' Report Finds LGBT Television Characters At Record High." *Huffington Post*. Huffington Post, 5 Oct. 2012. Web. 28 Apr. 2013.

2. Craig A. Rimmerman. *Gay Rights, Military Wrongs: Political Perspectives on Lesbians and Gays in the Military*. New York: Taylor, 1996. Print. 6.

3. Mark Thompson. "'Don't Ask, Don't Tell' Turns 15." *Time*. Time, 28 Jan. 2008. Web. 28 Apr. 2013.

4. John D'Emilio. *Sexual Politics, Sexual Communities*. Chicago: U of Chicago, 1983. Print. 286.

5. John Leland. "O.K., You're Gay. So? Where's My Grandchild?" *New York Times*. New York Times, 21 Dec. 2000. Web. 28 Apr. 2013.

CHAPTER 9. A NEW ERA IN GAY RIGHTS

1. Jesse McKinley. "California Couples Await Gay Marriage Ruling." *New York Times*. New York Times, 25 May 2009. Web. 28 Apr. 2013.

2. "Defining Marriage: Defense of Marriage Acts and Same-Sex Marriage Laws." *National Conference of State Legislatures*. National Conference of State Legislatures, 15 May 2013. Web. 22 May 2013.

3. Ibid.

4. "Gay Rights Backers See History in Obama's Stand. *Fox News*. Fox News, 11 May 2012. Web. 28 Apr. 2013.

5. "Mayor Defends Same-Sex Marriages." *CNN*. Cable News Network, 22 Feb 2004. Web. 28 Apr. 2013.

6. Jesse McKinley. "California Couples Await Gay Marriage Ruling." *New York Times*. New York Times, 25 May 2009. Web. 28 Apr. 2013.

7. "Hillary Clinton On Gay Rights Abroad." *Huffington Post*. Huffington Post, 6 Dec. 2012. Web. 28 Apr. 2013.

8. "March 2013 Post-ABC Poll—Same-Sex Marriage." *Washington Post*. Washington Post, 26 Mar. 2013. Web. 2 May 2013.

9. Marjorie Connelly. "Support for Gay Marriage Growing, but U.S. Remains Divided." *New York Times*. New York Times, 7 Dec. 2012. Web. 28 Apr. 2013.

10. "New Report Documents 'Decade of Progress' on Lesbian, Gay, Bisexual and Transgender Equality in America." *PR Newswire*. PR Newswire, 16 Dec. 2009. Web. 28 Apr. 2013.

INDEX

ABOUT THE AUTHOR

Stephanie Watson is a freelance writer based in Atlanta, Georgia. Over her more than 20-year career, she has written for television, radio, the Web, and print. Stephanie has authored or contributed to more than 30 books, including *Elvis Presley: Rock & Roll's King*, *Heath Ledger: Talented Actor*, and *Under Pressure: Handling the Stresses of Keeping Up*.

ABOUT THE CONSULTANT

Donald P. Haider-Markel is professor of political science and chair at the University of Kansas. His research and teaching is focused on the representation of interests in the policy process and the dynamics between public opinion and policy. He has authored or coauthored more than 45 refereed articles, multiple book chapters, and several books in a range of issue areas, including gay and lesbian civil rights, the environment, criminal justice, terrorism, and religion and culture wars. He has been the recipient or corecipient of grants from the EPA STAR program, the National Science Foundation, and the American Psychological Foundation.